Made in United States
Orlando, FL
31 August 2022

21799218R00067